OTABA

LETTERS for LUCARDO
the silent lord

IRON CIRCUS COMICS

strange and amazing

inquiry@ironcircus.com   www.ironcircus.com

Writer/Artist: Otava Heikkilä

Publisher: C. Spike Trotman

Editor: Andrea Purcell

Art Director: Matt Sheridan

Book Design/Print Technician: Beth Scorzato

Proofreader: Abby Lerhke

Published by
Iron Circus Comics
329 West 18th Street, Suite 604
Chicago, IL 60616
ironcircus.com

First Edition: October 2022

ISBN: 978-1-63899-101-4

Printed in Thailand

LETTERS FOR LUCARDO: THE SILENT LORD

Publisher's Cataloging-In-Publication Data
(Prepared by The Donohue Group, Inc.)

Names: Heikkilä, Otava, author, artist. | Spike, 1978- publisher. |
    Purcell, Andrea, editor. | Sheridan, Matt, 1978- designer. | Rasmussen-
    Silverstein, Rhiannon, designer.
Title: Letters for Lucardo. [Book 3], The silent lord / Otava Heikkilä
    [writer/artist] ; [publisher: C. Spike Trotman ; editor: Andrea Purcell
    ; art designer: Matt Sheridan ; book design/print technician, Rhiannon
    Rasmussen-Silverstein ; proofreader, Abby Lehrke].
Other Titles: Silent lord
Description: First edition. | Chicago, IL : Iron Circus Comics, 2022.
Identifiers: ISBN 9781638991014 (trade paperback)
Subjects: LCSH: Older gay men–Comic books, strips, etc. | Vampires–Comic
    books, strips, etc. | Terminally ill–Comic books, strips, etc. |
    LCGFT: Graphic novels. | Erotic fiction.
Classification: LCC PN6790.F53 H453 2022 | DDC 741.594897–dc23

EXCUSE ME!
WAIT!

THERE'S NO ADDRESS.

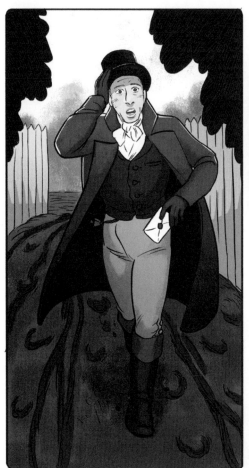

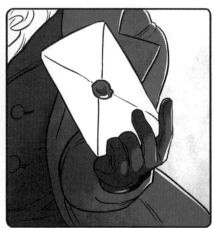

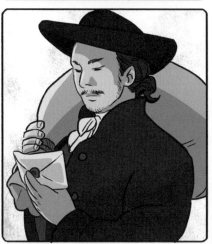

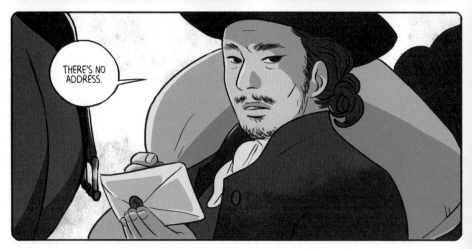

THERE ISN'T.
IF YOU COULD SEND IT NEVER-THELESS?
ADDRESS.
OR I'M NOT SENDING IT ANYWHERE.
...TO THE NIGHT COURT IN THE HOLY SEAT?

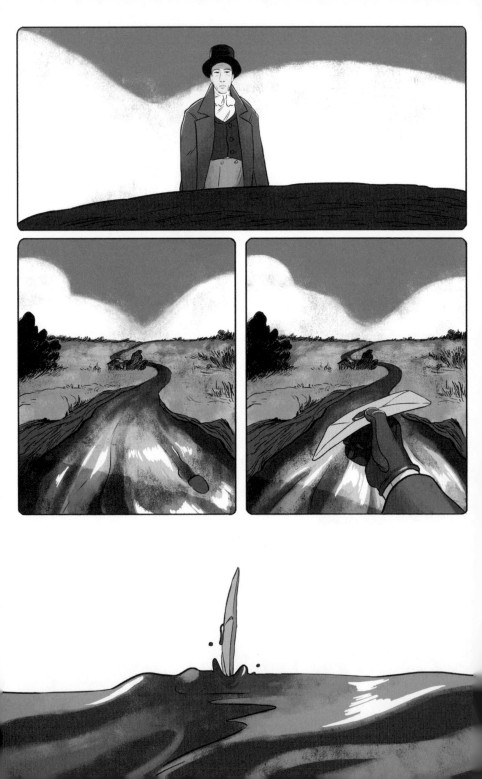

BOOK THREE: THE SILENT LORD

13

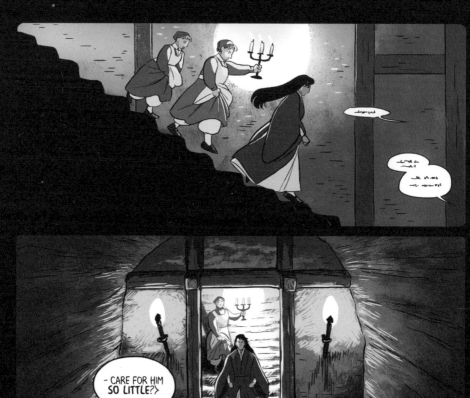

- CARE FOR HIM
SO LITTLE?>

<THAT YOU WILL
PUT HIM THROUGH
THIS **MAGNITUDE** OF
SUFFERING?>

YOU DID THIS TO ME TOO! YOU DID THIS TO US ALL!
I WAS YOUNG, A **FOOL**!
IF I COULD TURN BACK TIME, INSTEAD OF BEING **TETHERED** IN IT!

<LUCARDO, WHAT HAVE YOU DONE?>

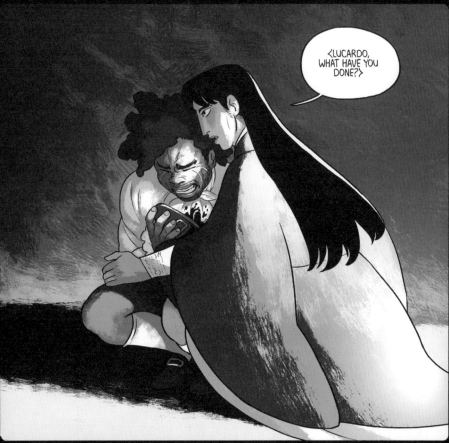

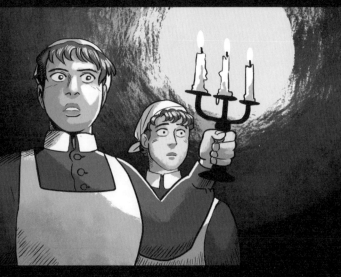

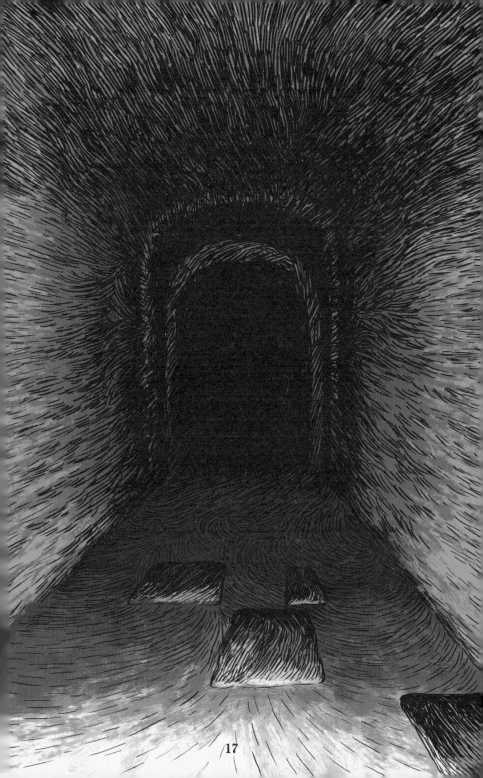

POK

EDMUND!
ÄLÄ MENE SINNE!

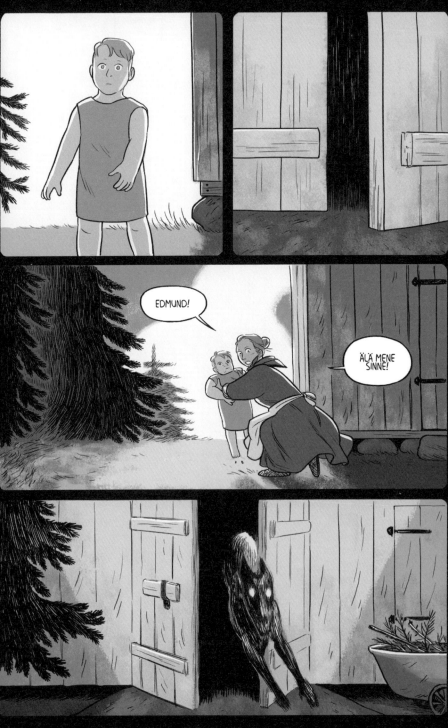

AH!

WAAH
WAAAH
WAAAH
WAAAH

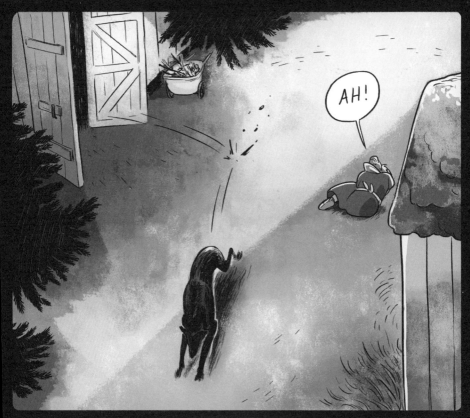

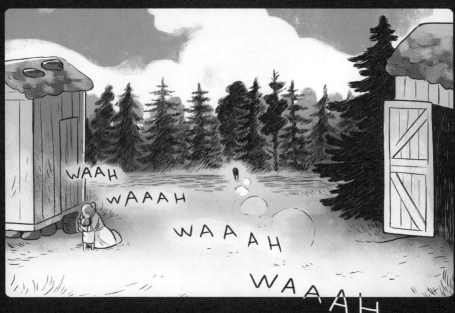

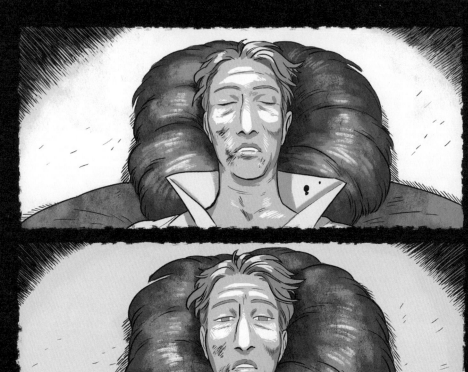

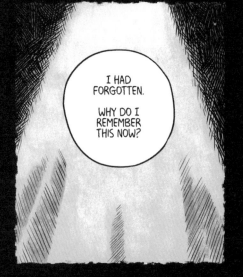

I HAD
FORGOTTEN.

WHY DO I
REMEMBER
THIS NOW?

I THOUGHT
IT WOULD
BE FITTING.

I MUST HAVE BEEN THREE.
I FELT BAD AFTER THROWING THE STONE.
WHY?
IT LOOKED FRIGHTENED, EVEN THOUGH I WAS A CHILD.
THERE'S NO WAY I COULD'VE HARMED IT.

EVERYONE TAUGHT YOU THE BEASTS
ATE CHILDREN, AND TO STAY AWAY
FROM THE FOREST.

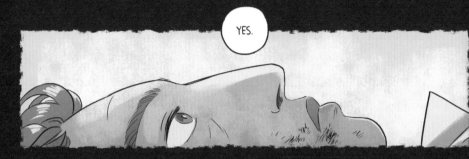

THEY WERE RIGHT.

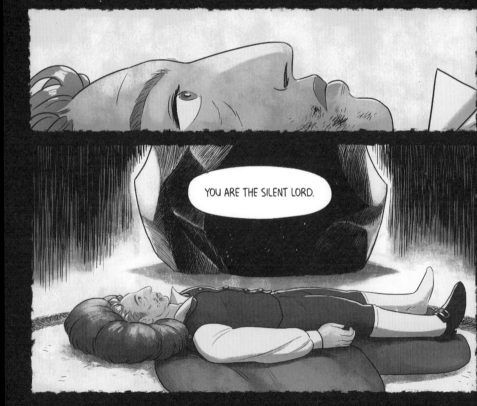

YOU ARE BARELY HOLDING ON. IT'S UGLY TO LOOK AT. WHICH OF MY CHILDREN HAS LEFT YOU TO DIE IN MY PRESENCE?

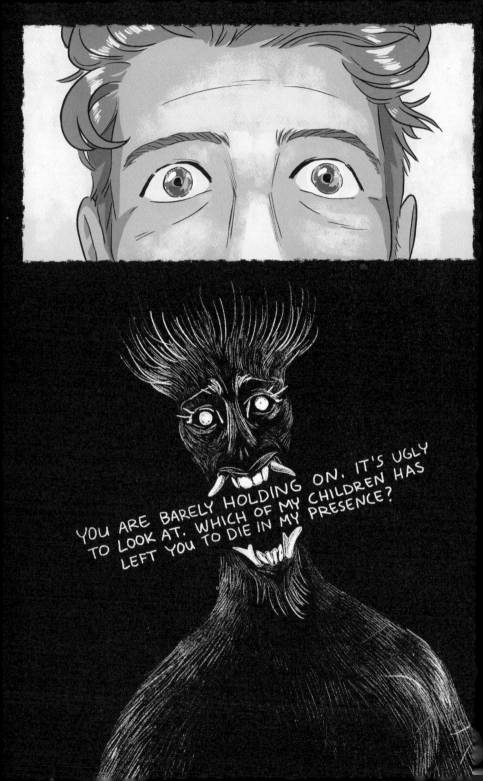

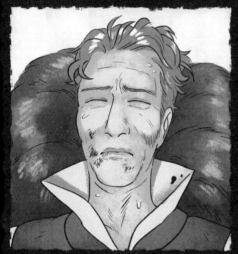
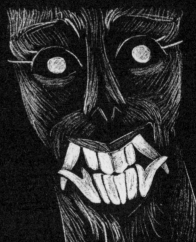

OH, IT'S ISSHAN'S SON. WHAT A SURPRISE. HE WISHES ME TO SAVE YOU FROM DEATH'S DOOR. WHAT DO YOU THINK, EDMUND?

YOU DO NOT WISH FOR MY GIFT.

I'M SORRY.
I FIND IT AMUSING
DO YOU KNOW EVERY MEMBER OF THIS "COURT" GROVELED FOR MY GIFTS? GROVELING DOGGIES.
THEY WOULD DO ANYTHING FOR IT.

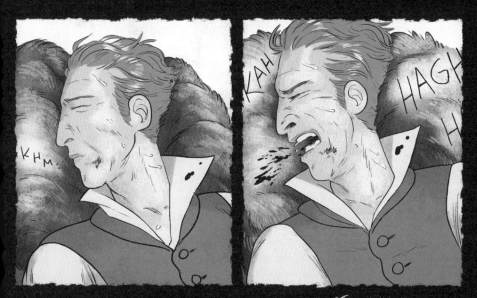

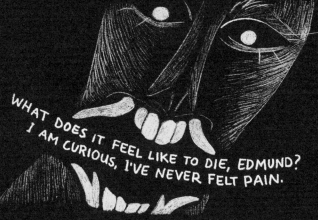

WHAT DOES IT FEEL LIKE TO DIE, EDMUND? I AM CURIOUS, I'VE NEVER FELT PAIN.

I AM VERY CURIOUS, ED. YOU MUST KNOW THE STORY OF ME. HOW I'M BOUND HERE IN THE FOREST.

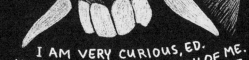

MY ONLY SOLACE FROM BOREDOM ARE THE EYES OF MY CHILDREN. IF ONLY THEY CAME TO VISIT ME, EVERY ONCE IN A WHILE. WHY DON'T YOU VISIT MORE OFTEN, CHILDREN?
ED. YOU COULD BE MY CHILD. YOU COULD COME VISIT ME. YOU COULD SHOW ME WHAT IT FEELS LIKE TO BE SO FEEBLE AND OLD. I'M SORRY, IS THAT A RUDE THING TO POINT OUT? IT WOULDN'T HAVE TO BE LIKE THAT.

WHAT HAVE YOU DONE?
WHAT IS IT THAT YOU WANT?
IT CAN BE ANYTHING, EDMUND.

BEAUTY? YOUTH?
PASSIONATE LOVERS?
I CAN OFFER IT TO YOU-
NO...
YOU ONLY NEED TO GIVE A PIECE OF YOURSELF TO ME.

NO!

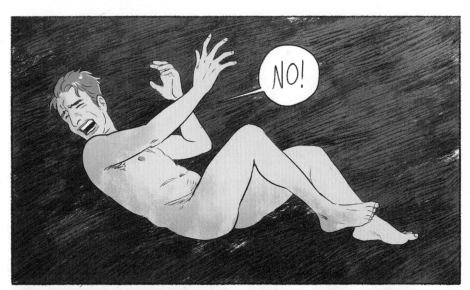

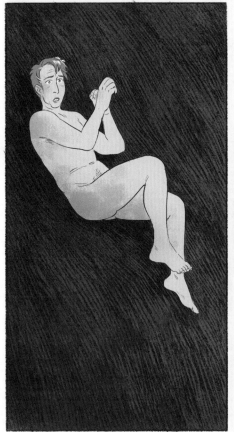

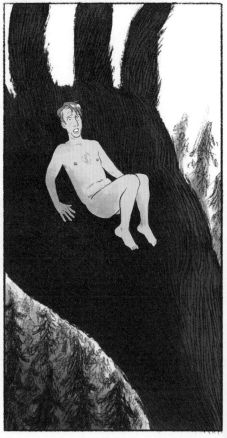

"NO"?
YOU MISUNDERSTAND, EDMUND
I WILL PLUCK WHATEVER RIPE BERRY I WANT OUT OF MY GARDEN,
AND ONCE YOU'RE RUNNING ON MY FAST LITTLE LEGS
YOU WILL COME TO ME, YOU WILL ALWAYS COME TO ME—
AND WE WILL LAUGH AND PLAY TOGETHER
UNTIL THE WORLD ENDS

YOU HURT THEM!
THEY WORSHIP YOU, AND YOU HURT THEM!

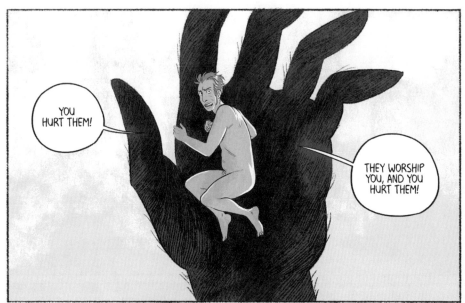

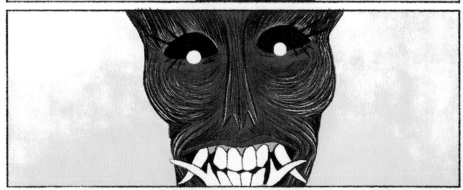

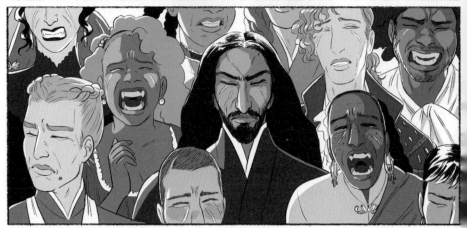

PLIP
PLIP
PLIP
PLIP

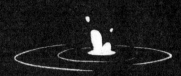

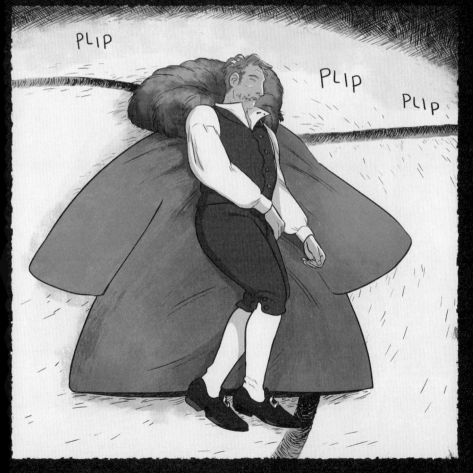

PLIP
PLIP

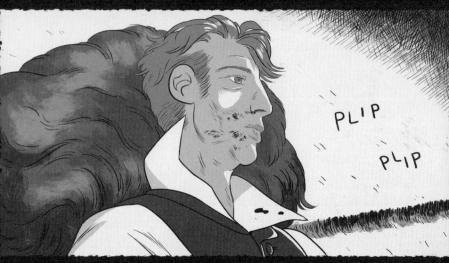

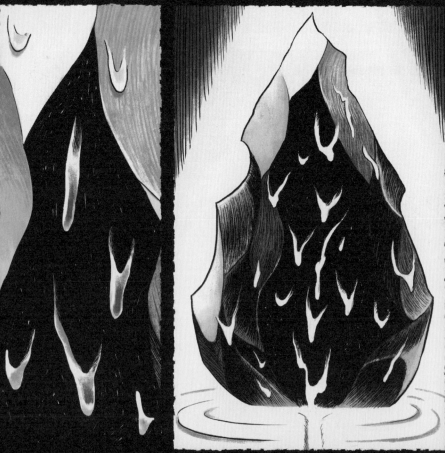

PLIP
PLIP
DRINK.
PLIP

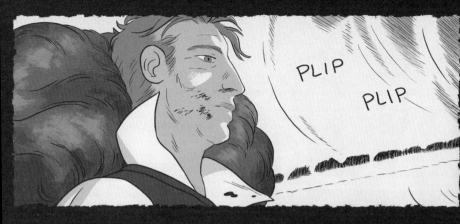

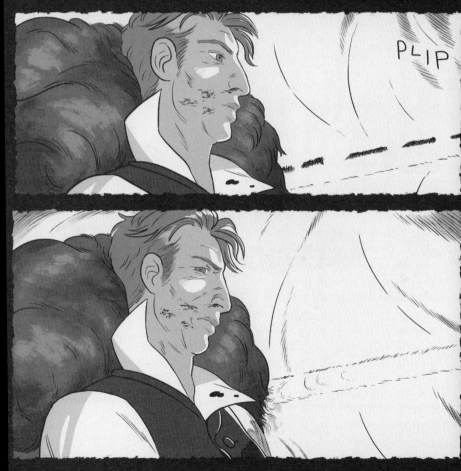

DRINK

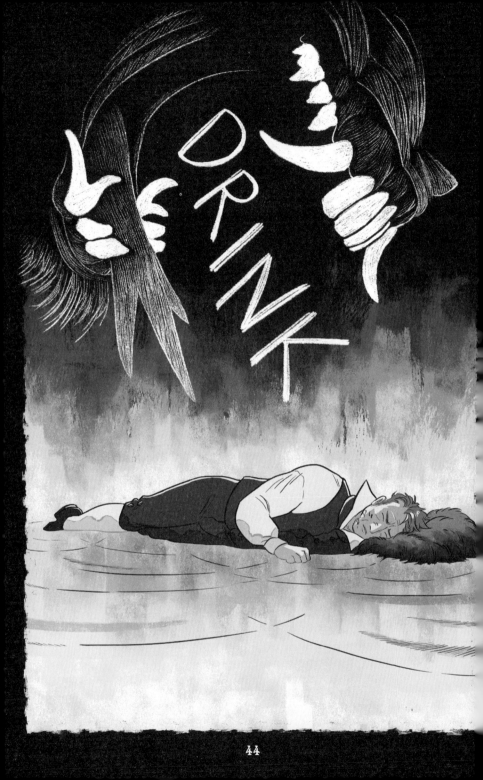

WE'L HAVE ON W ROO AT

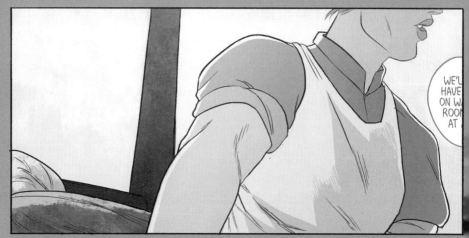

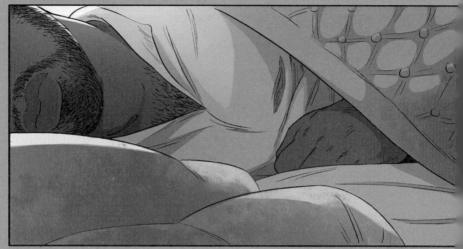

I CAN CONFIRM HE'S CHANGING, BUT WE ARE GOING TO HAVE TO WAIT AND SEE HOW.
EDMUND HASN'T YET BEEN AWARE ENOUGH TO SPEAK TO ME.
HE SPOKE TO ME.
YES, LUC, BUT HE'S NOT WELL ENOUGH TO HOLD A CONVERSATION YET.

UNTIL THEN WE WON'T KNOW THE DETAILS OF WHAT TRANSPIRED BETWEEN EDMUND AND THE LORD,
UNLESS ONE OF US WANTS TO TALK TO **HIM** INSTEAD.
IT IS DONE, THEN.
DOCTOR, ARE YOU ABLE TO HELP MISTER FIEDLER THROUGH THIS?
I UNDERSTAND YOU ARE THE ONLY ONE WITH THE EXPERIENCE OF HELPING SOMEBODY THROUGH SUCH AN...
UNORTHODOX TRANSITION WITHIN THE COURT.

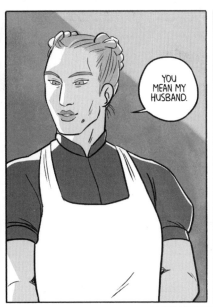

YOU MEAN MY HUSBAND.

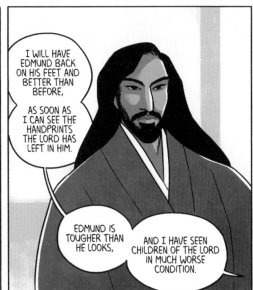

I WILL HAVE EDMUND BACK ON HIS FEET AND BETTER THAN BEFORE,

AS SOON AS I CAN SEE THE HANDPRINTS THE LORD HAS LEFT IN HIM.

EDMUND IS TOUGHER THAN HE LOOKS,

AND I HAVE SEEN CHILDREN OF THE LORD IN MUCH WORSE CONDITION.

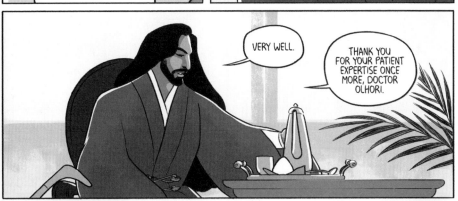

VERY WELL.

THANK YOU FOR YOUR PATIENT EXPERTISE ONCE MORE, DOCTOR OLHORI.

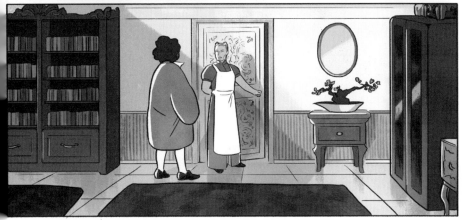

LUCARDO.
HOW ARE YOU FEELING?
WELL, MY BOYFRIEND IS DYING, I'VE GOT HIS BLOOD ON ALL MY CLOTHES,
AND EARLIER I LEFT HIM IN A COLD CHAMBER WITH THE SILENT LORD,
AND JUST PACED OUTSIDE WAITING FOR ALL THE WORST HORRIBLE NEWS,
BUT OTHER THAN THAT I'M WELL, DOC.
HOW ABOUT YOU?

I AM ALSO WELL, THANK YOU,
THOUGH I'M WONDERING IF ONE PATIENT IS GOING NEGLECTED IN THE CHAOS OF IT ALL.
HE SEEMS TO BE COCOONING IN DIRTY BLANKETS AND HUMOR, TO COPE.
YEAH, WELL.
TELL ME WHEN YOU FIND THE CURE TO HEART-ACHE, DOCTOR.
I'LL LET YOU BE THE FIRST ONE TO KNOW.

HEY.
WHICH ONE OF YOU NUMBSKULLS WAS SUPPOSED TO WATCH HIM?
LULUUU!
YOUR BOY-FRIEND WOKE UUUP!

LOOK AT YOUR BEARD!
I HAVE A BEARD?
LIKE AN ANCIENT WOODSMAN.

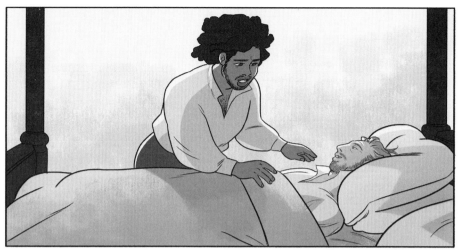

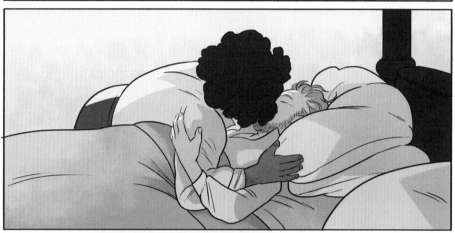

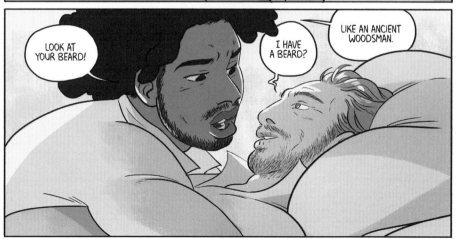

HOW DO YOU FEEL, SWEETHEART?
I-
ARE YOU HUNGRY?
IS ANYTHING HURTING?
I CAN BRING YOU PAIN MEDICINE.
I'M NOT HURTING, LOVE.
...GLAD TO HEAR THAT, YOU HAVE NO IDEA.
THERE'S DINNER BEING PREPARED RIGHT NOW, I'LL GET YOU A PORTION-
WE'LL GET YOU FULL OF GOOD FOOD, AND YOU'LL REST FOR AS LONG AS YOU NEED TO...

...HONEY. ARE YOU SURE YOU'RE OKAY?
...JUST A DIZZY SPELL, THAT'S ALL.
I SHOULDN'T PUSH YOU.
YOU MUST BE TIRED.

WE'RE NOT GOING TO SEE A LOT OF CHANGES A WEEK AND A HALF AFTER THE RITUAL.
THAT'S TO BE EXPECTED,
BUT I AM TENTATIVELY OPTIMISTIC ABOUT EDMUND'S RECOVERY.
THE SHIFTER'S LUNG HAS GONE INTO REMISSION,
WHICH IS VERY GOOD, YES.
NOW I MUST ASK THAT YOU ALL GIVE EDMUND THE TIME AND SPACE HE NEEDS TO **ACCLIMATIZE**.
I'M LOOKING AT THE FOUR OF YOU IN THE BACK.
NO FUNNY BUSINESS ON EDMUND'S BEHALF.
YES?
YES.

WE ALL ENTERED THE LORD'S CONTRACT ILL-PREPARED BUT WANTING IT.
IT'S MY UNDERSTANDING EDMUND WASN'T GIVEN THE CHOICE.
PLEASE KEEP THAT IN MIND AS A NEW CHILD IS INTRODUCED TO OUR MIDST, AND TREAT HIM ACCORDINGLY.
WE ARE ALL VERY OLD AND FULL OF HINDSIGHT. HE IS NOT.
HOW ARE YOU FEELING, EDMUND?

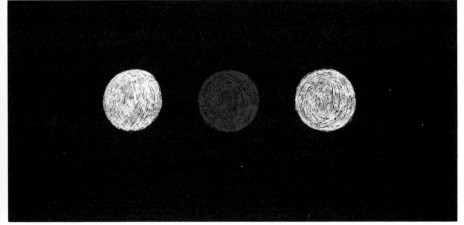

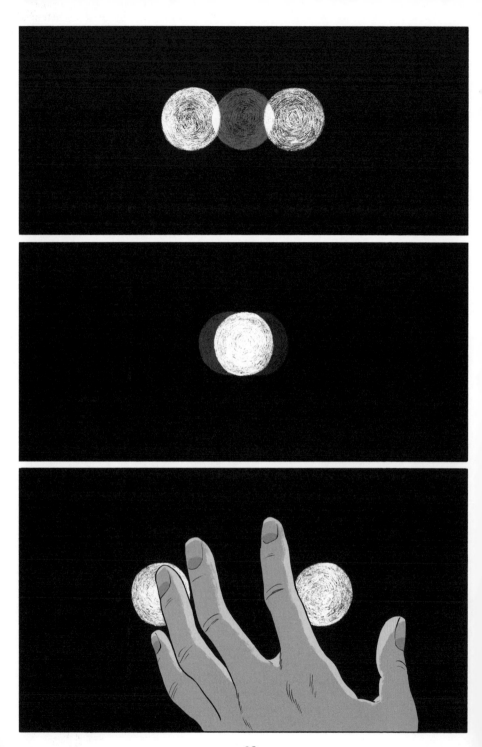

HAH
HAAH
HA...

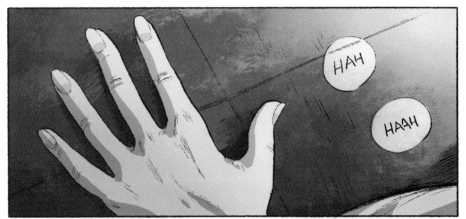

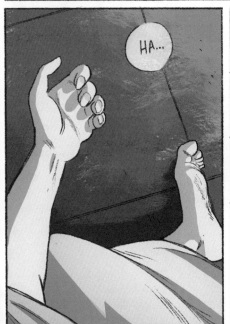

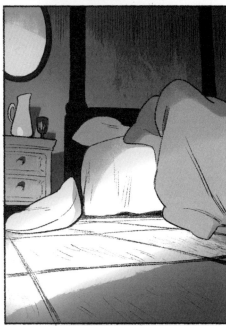

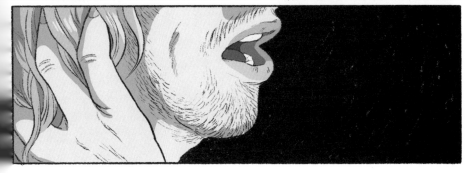

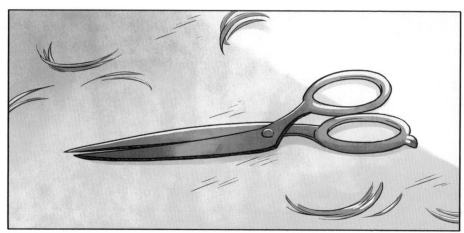

I TRIED TO... UH
SWEETHEART.
IT'S OKAY, WE CAN FIX THIS.

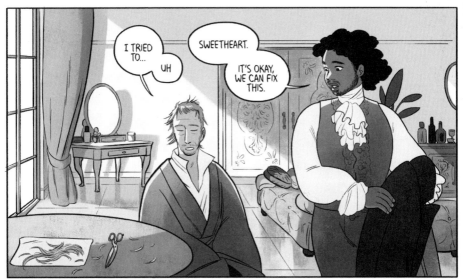

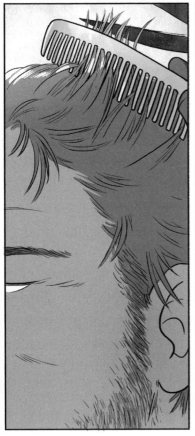

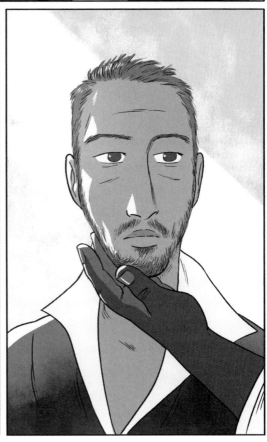

IT'S HARD ENOUGH CUTTING SOMEBODY ELSE'S HAIR.
HAHA
BUT LOOK HOW HANDSOME YOU TURNED OUT!
THANK YOU FOR THE HELP, DEAR.
HOW ARE WE FEELING ABOUT THE BEARD?
SHOULD IT STAY?
DO YOU LIKE IT?
I THINK IT'S **CRIMINALLY** HANDSOME.
LIKE THE SILVER FOX OF MY DREAMS.
HEH

LUC...
ARE YOU OKAY?

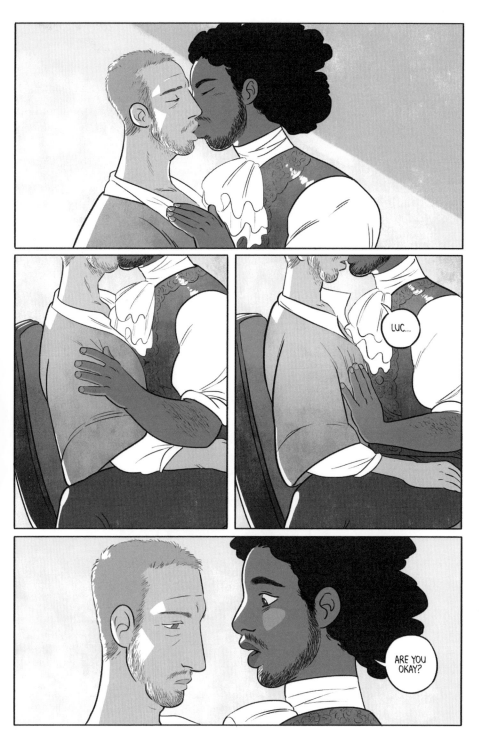

AM I HURTING YOU?
NO, LOVE,
YOU DIDN'T HURT ME.
I'M JUST...
TIRED.

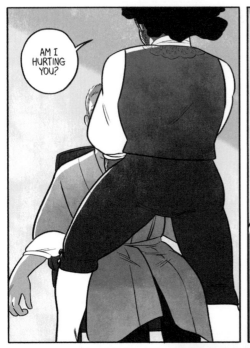

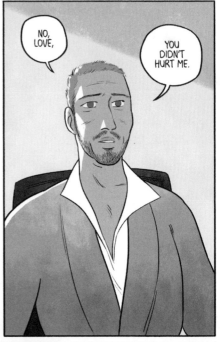

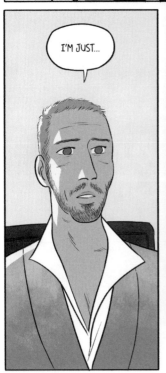

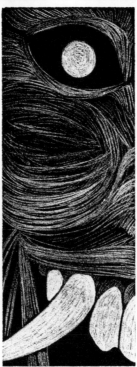

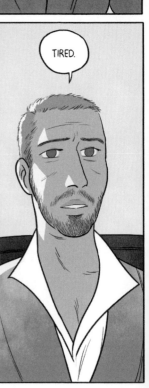

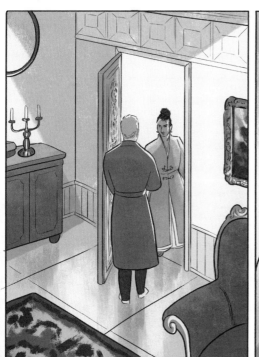

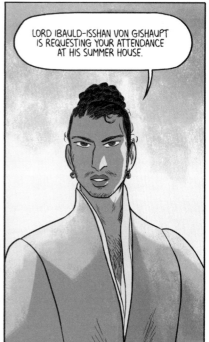

LORD IBAULD-ISSHAN VON GISHAUPT IS REQUESTING YOUR ATTENDANCE AT HIS SUMMER HOUSE.

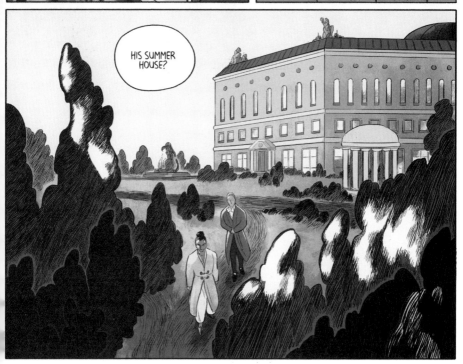

HIS SUMMER HOUSE?

BACKYARD.

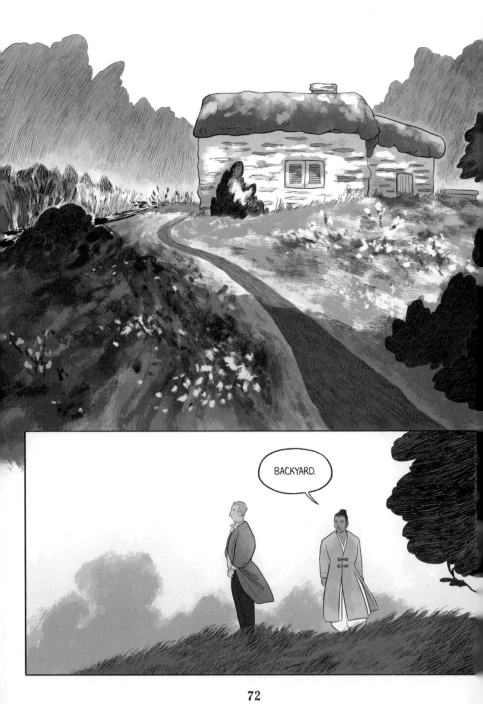

GOOD MORNING, MISTER FIEDLER.
MY LORD.
WOULD YOU LIKE SOME TEA?

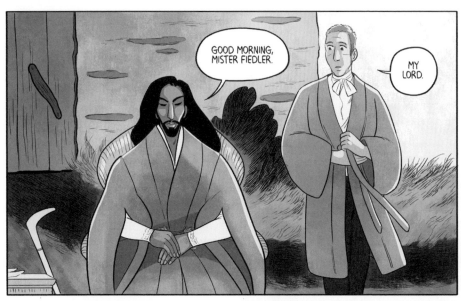

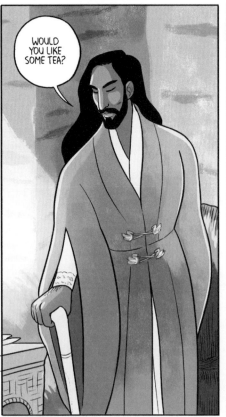

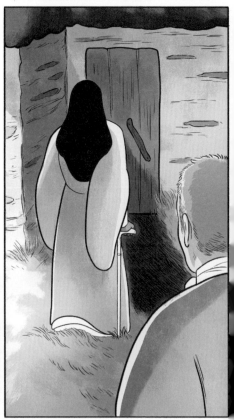

I LIKE THE COTTAGE, MY LORD.
HRMM.
A SENTIMENTAL REMNANT.
A MEMORY OF A MEMORY.
HOW ARE YOU DOING, EDMUND?

NOT GREAT.
WHAT IS HE?

I DO NOT KNOW THE ANSWER TO THAT,
BUT I'LL TELL YOU WHAT I KNOW.
I MET THE SILENT LORD IN THE WILDERNESS A THOUSAND YEARS AGO.

HE WAS BEAUTIFUL, WISE AND IMMORTAL.
HE WAS EAGER TO SHARE HIS GIFTS TO ME, AND I WAS EAGER TO RECEIVE THEM.
BUT HE'S NOT A HUMAN OR AN ANIMAL OR ANYTHING THAT FEELS PAIN AND DIES.
WHATEVER FORCE TIED HIM TO THAT FOREST IN THE BEGINNING OF TIME UNDERSTOOD THE SILENT LORD'S NATURE,
AND RIGHTLY BANISHED HIM.

HE WOULD ALWAYS SAY IT WAS ME THAT HE'D BEEN WAITING FOR SINCE THE START OF TIME,
MY SPECIAL HEART OF HEARTS! YOU ARE **ALWAYS** MINE!
BUT ANYONE COULD HAVE STRAYED INTO HIS DOMAIN AND FALLEN HIS VICTIM.
MANY **DID**, I FOUND OUT LATER.
I... **ENDURED** THROUGH MY TIME INDULGING HIM.
HE HAD NO WAY OUT BUT MY EYES, AND NO COMPANY BUT MY BODY.

BUT YOU GOT OUT SOMEHOW.

THE ROCKS HE'S LAID ON FOREVER ARE PART OF HIM NOW.

I LEARNED THIS BY ACCIDENT, – SPEAKING TO THE STONE I WAS SPEAKING TO HIM WITHOUT LETTING HIM NEAR ME.

I ASKED HIM FOR A SHOW OF STRENGTH.

OF COURSE HE WAS ONLY HAPPY TO PLAY ALONG.

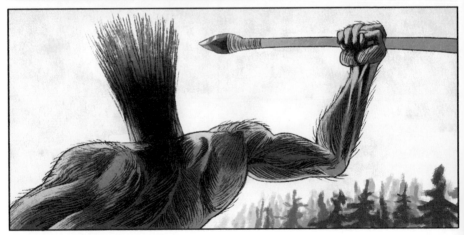

IT TOOK ME OVER A YEAR TO FIND THE PIECE HE'D THROWN. WHEN I FOUND IT, I WEPT WITH RELIEF.
I COULD FINALLY STAY AWAY FROM HIM FOR MONTHS, YEARS, -
CENTURIES, WITHOUT BREAKING OUR BARGAIN.
IT WAS A MIRACLE, TO ME.
I MADE OTHERS VIEW IT AS A MIRACLE, AS WELL.
I HAD TIME, - FAR MORE THAN THE REIGNING KINGS AND QUEENS.
I CREATED THE NIGHT COURT, TO STAND BESIDE THE DAY COURT OF THE HUMANS.
I CREATED THE FAITH AS WELL. MY FAMILY WOULD ALWAYS BE SAFE WITHIN THESE WALLS.
YOU WEREN'T ALONE.
YOUR FAMILY...
WERE THEY THE PEOPLE WHO HAD FOUND HIM IN THE WILDER-NESS AS WELL?
A FEW OF THEM.
BUT A LOT OF US,
IT PAINS ME TO SAY,
I INTRODUCED TO THE CURSE, MYSELF.
I WAS YOUNG, AND FOOLISH, AND ALONE.
I WANTED MY LIFE BACK, AND I WANTED A FAMILY.

YOU CREATED A STORY TO KEEP YOUR FAMILY SAFE.
THAT THE SILENT LORD IS A GOD, AND YOUR FAMILY CAN DIVINE WITH HIM DIRECTLY.
STORIES LIVE LONGER THAN BLOODLINES.
BUT THERE'S NOTHING TO DIVINE.
HE ONLY HURTS YOU.
TELLING THIS STORY KEEPS MY FAMILY SAFE FROM HUMANS AND SILENT LORD BOTH.
IN THIS WAY, HE IS OUR PROTECTION AS WELL.

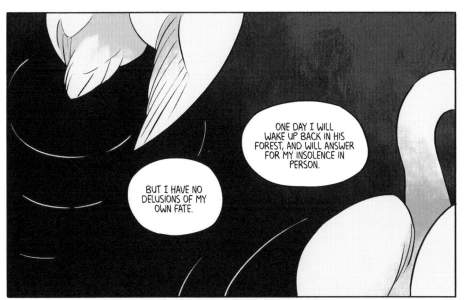

ONE DAY I WILL WAKE UP BACK IN HIS FOREST, AND WILL ANSWER FOR MY INSOLENCE IN PERSON.

BUT I HAVE NO DELUSIONS OF MY OWN FATE.

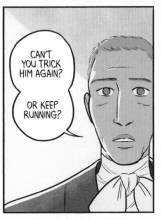

CAN'T YOU TRICK HIM AGAIN?

OR KEEP RUNNING?

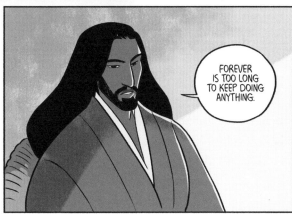

FOREVER IS TOO LONG TO KEEP DOING ANYTHING.

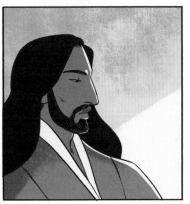

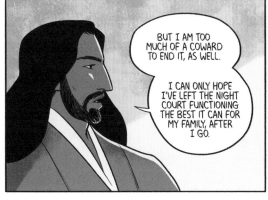

BUT I AM TOO MUCH OF A COWARD TO END IT, AS WELL.

I CAN ONLY HOPE I'VE LEFT THE NIGHT COURT FUNCTIONING THE BEST IT CAN FOR MY FAMILY, AFTER I GO.

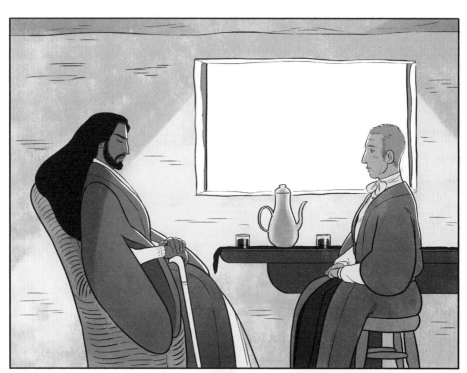

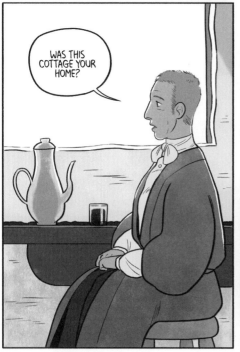

WAS THIS COTTAGE YOUR HOME?

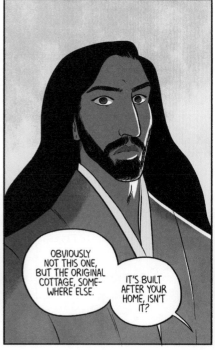

OBVIOUSLY NOT THIS ONE, BUT THE ORIGINAL COTTAGE, SOME- WHERE ELSE.

IT'S BUILT AFTER YOUR HOME, ISN'T IT?

IT WAS THE PLACE...
THAT WELCOMED ME,
WHEN I DESERVED IT THE LEAST.

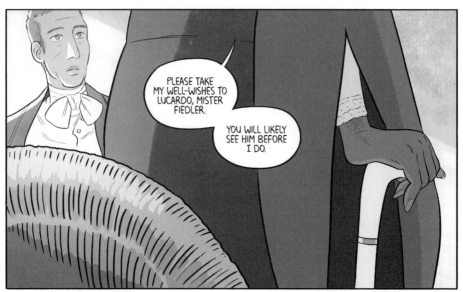

PLEASE TAKE MY WELL-WISHES TO LUCARDO, MISTER FIEDLER.

YOU WILL LIKELY SEE HIM BEFORE I DO.

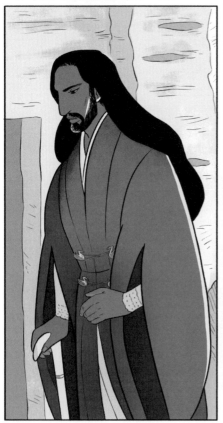

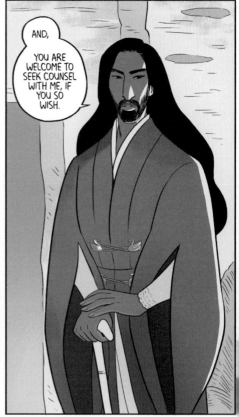

AND,

YOU ARE WELCOME TO SEEK COUNSEL WITH ME, IF YOU SO WISH.

THE BEGINNING IS A TERRIBLE TIME TO BE ALONE WITH YOUR THOUGHTS.

UPPER LEFT CANINE.
AT THE PARTY?
YES.
I, UH, BIT INTO SOMETHING.

NOTHING TO WORRY ABOUT, EDMUND.

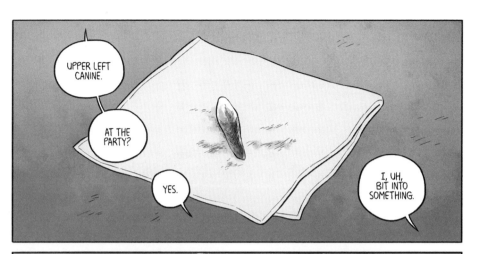

ARE THERE ANY OTHER CHANGES YOU FEEL COMFORTABLE SHARING?
NOT THAT I CAN THINK OF.
...
ACTUALLY, I, UH, NOTICED MY VISION IS GETTING BLURRY...
BLURRY?

WHEN I...
WHEN I WEAR THESE, I FIND IT HARD TO READ NOW.
IT'S EASIER IF I DON'T WEAR THEM.
YOU ARE SEEING BETTER WITHOUT YOUR GLASSES?
I SUPPOSE SO.
WELL, GOOD!
I WILL NOT PRESCRIBE ANYTHING FOR THAT, I THINK.

YOU WILL LIKELY LOSE A FEW MORE TEETH IN THE UPCOMING WEEKS.
IT'S A PERFECTLY NORMAL PART OF THE PROCESS.
AM I...
YES?
GROWING NEW ONES?
YOU ARE.
AND WHAT, AH,
OTHER NEW THINGS WILL I EXPECT TO GROW?

IT WILL DEPEND A LITTLE ON YOUR INDIVIDUAL CIRCUMSTANCES.
THERE MAY BE CHANGES TO YOUR SMELL AND APPETITE. SOME OF US HAVE AN INCREASE IN BOTH.
OTHERS DON'T.
YOUR BEARD MAY GROW IN A LITTLE MORE FIERCELY.
DO YOU NEED A MOMENT, EDMUND?

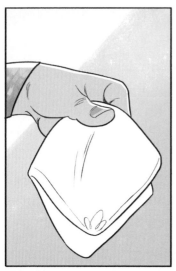

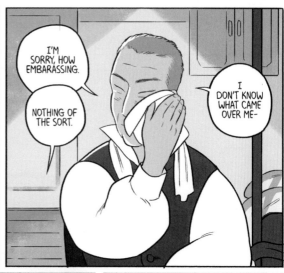

I'M SORRY, HOW EMBARASSING.

NOTHING OF THE SORT.

I DON'T KNOW WHAT CAME OVER ME-

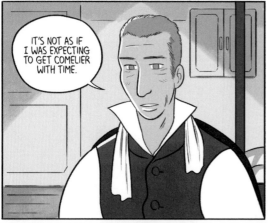

IT'S NOT AS IF I WAS EXPECTING TO GET COMELIER WITH TIME.

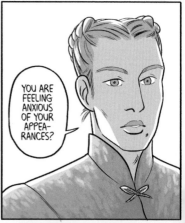

YOU ARE FEELING ANXIOUS OF YOUR APPEA-RANCES?

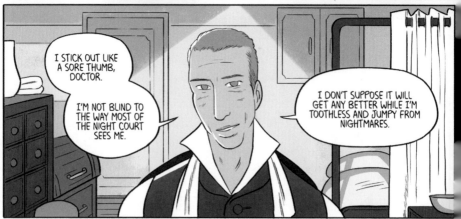

I STICK OUT LIKE A SORE THUMB, DOCTOR.

I'M NOT BLIND TO THE WAY MOST OF THE NIGHT COURT SEES ME.

I DON'T SUPPOSE IT WILL GET ANY BETTER WHILE I'M TOOTHLESS AND JUMPY FROM NIGHTMARES.

I SEE. YES. THE NIGHT COURT, AS A BODY, CAN FEEL CAPRICIOUS AND TESTING.
THE MOTIVES BEHIND THE POSTURING ARE BEYOND ME.
SOME KIND OF INITIATION GAME?
YOU WILL GET THROUGH IT.
THE WORST IS BEHIND NOW.
PERSONALLY, I HAVE A FONDNESS FOR SORE THUMBS IN OUR COMMU-NITY.
I'D LIKE TO SAY IT'S MY CARETAKING INSTINCT, BUT I JUST HATE TO SEE THINGS GET TOO **AGREEABLE**.
-Teeth beginning to change starting with upper left canine
- eyesight corrected, no lon
- emotionally low, stricken
Meeting Sorin
EDMUND, I'D LIKE YOU TO MEET SOMEBODY TONIGHT.
OH?
OH, YES. LET'S CALL IT MY PRESCRIPTION TO YOUR CURRENT AILMENTS.

HERE WE ARE.

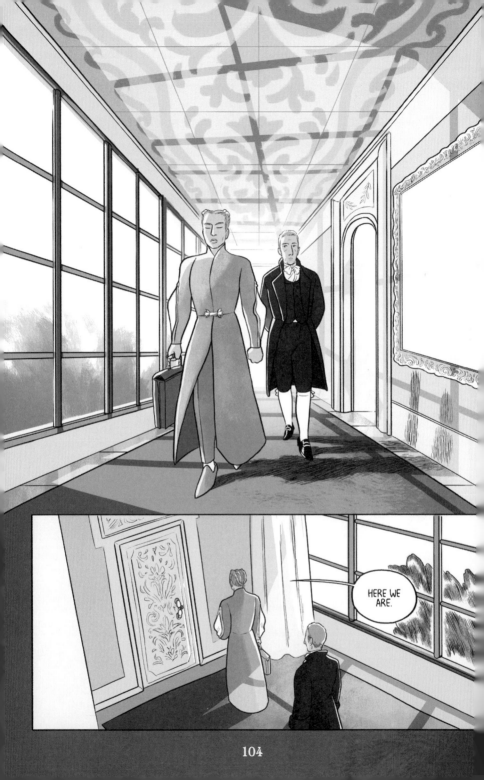

MEGJÖTTEM.
GÉZA, SZÖRNYEN HIÁNYOZTÁL.
ELKEZDHETJÜK AZ ÜNNEPLÉST?
NEM, MÉG NEM.
BUT SOME-BODY ELSE IS VISITING US.

EDMUND, THIS IS MY HUSBAND, SORIN.
SORIN, THIS IS THE NEWEST MEMBER OF THE NIGHT COURT.
EDMUND FIEDLER.
EDMUND.
NICE TO MEET YOU!

OH!
OH, GOD, SORRY-
HAHA. DO NOT WORRY.
HUMANS TOOK IT SO LONG AGO.
IT'S BEEN HUNDREDS OF YEARS.
HUMANS-?
WITH A STEEL TRAP.

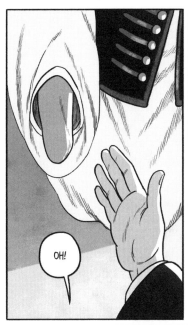

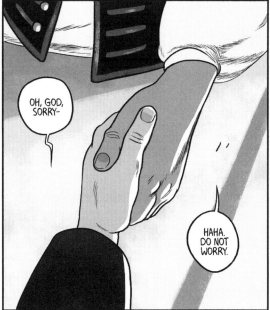

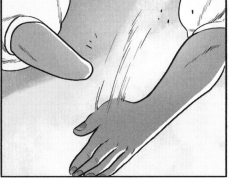

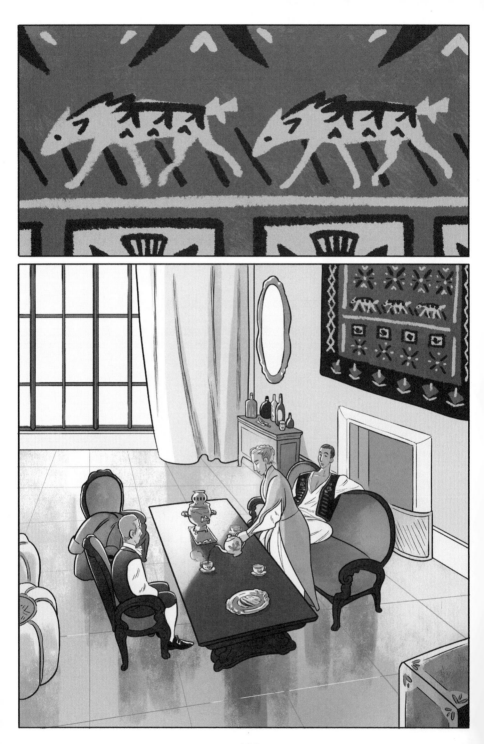

S-SO, HOW DID YOU TWO MEET?

GÉZA CAME TO FIND ME IN THE FOREST.
I'M SORRY, IN THE FOREST?
MY FOREST.
I WAS LIVING ALONE FOR A LONG TIME.

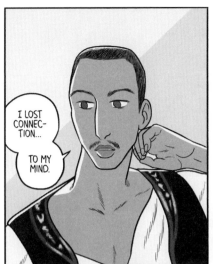

I LOST CONNEC-TION...

TO MY MIND.

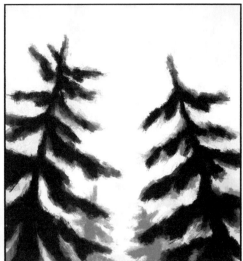

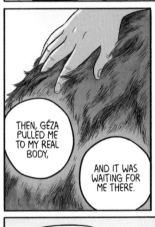

THEN, GÉZA PULLED ME TO MY REAL BODY,

AND IT WAS WAITING FOR ME THERE.

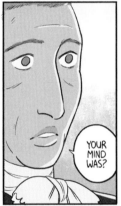

YOUR MIND WAS?

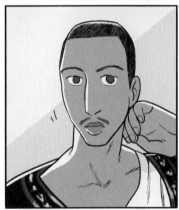

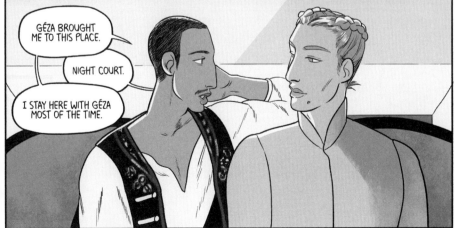

GÉZA BROUGHT ME TO THIS PLACE.

NIGHT COURT.

I STAY HERE WITH GÉZA MOST OF THE TIME.

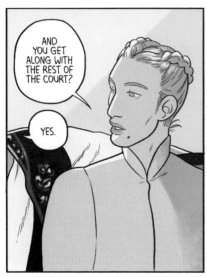

AND YOU GET ALONG WITH THE REST OF THE COURT?

YES.

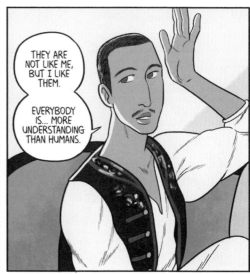

THEY ARE NOT LIKE ME, BUT I LIKE THEM.

EVERYBODY IS... MORE UNDERSTANDING THAN HUMANS.

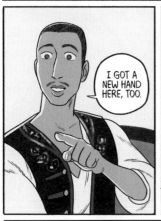

I GOT A NEW HAND HERE, TOO.

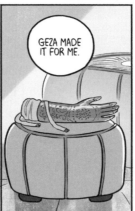

GEZA MADE IT FOR ME.

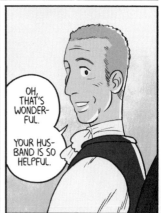

OH, THAT'S WONDERFUL.

YOUR HUSBAND IS SO HELPFUL.

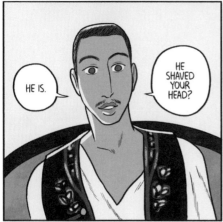

HE IS.

HE SHAVED YOUR HEAD?

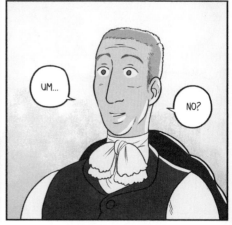

UM...

NO?

112

I DIDN'T SHAVE MISTER FIEDLER'S HEAD.
BUT I DID BRING HIM HERE, SO THAT HE COULD MEET SOMEBODY -
WHO NAVIGATES THE COURT A LITTLE DIFFERENTLY.
EDMUND IS ALSO FROM THE FOREST?
I- AH, NO... THOUGH I WAS BORN IN A FORESTY AREA.
I WAS TOO.
WE ARE A LITTLE SIMILAR,
FORESTY AND HAIR-LESS.
I GUESS THAT'S TRUE.

WHEN I CAME HERE, I WAS ALL ALONE.
THERE WAS ONLY GÉZA FOR ME.
I FEARED IT WAS A MISTAKE.
I MISSED MY FOREST,
AND EVEN MY MIND WHEN IT HADN'T BELONGED TO ME.
I STARTED OVER, A STRANGER.
IN TIME I REALISED IT WAS STILL ME, JUST IN A NEW WAY.
AND I STILL VISIT MY FOREST SOMETIMES.
EVEN THOUGH MASTER IBAULD HATES IT AND WANTS IT TO STOP.
HE'S A GROUCHY ELDER.
HE DISAPPROVES OF MY WAYS.
HE DISAPPROVES OF MY WAYS, TOO.

WE **ARE** THE SAME!
HAHA
VISITING A FOREST SEEMS HARMLESS TO ME.
HAHA! I ATE MANY PEOPLE.
OH!

THOSE DAYS ARE BEHIND YOU NOW.
THOSE DAYS ARE BEHIND US NOW!
HA
HA HA
HA!

SWEETHEART—

I HEARD YOU'RE WITH THE DOC,-
IS EVERYTHING OKAY?

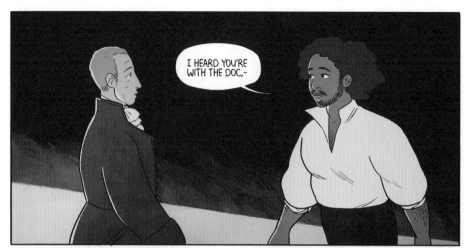

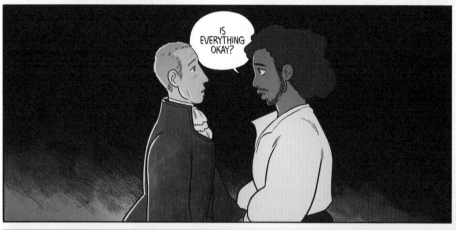

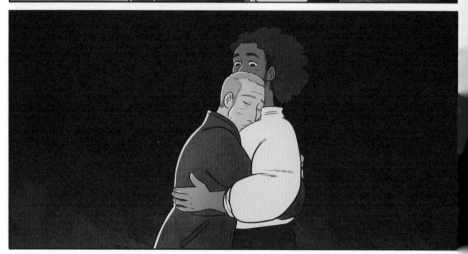

I SAW GÉZA'S HUSBAND.
SORIN.
HE'S A QUIRKY FELLOW.
ISN'T HE? DID YOU GET ALONG?
WE DID.

DID HE SHOW YOU HIS ACCESSORIES?
HIS ARM?
SURE, THE ARM.
I HEARD THE WHOLE STORY BEHIND IT.
YOU DON'T HAVE TO WORK VERY HARD TO BREAK THE ICE WITH HIM.
HEH.
I JUST NEED A MOMENT.
JUST LIKE THIS.

IT'S OKAY.
IT'S OKAY.
YOU'RE SAFE. I'M HERE.

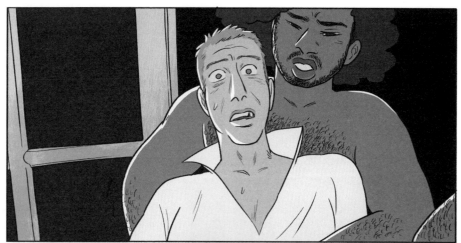

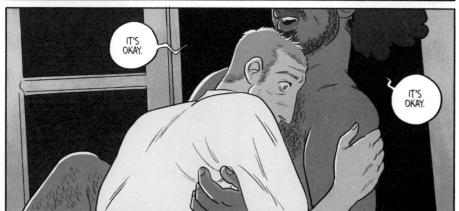

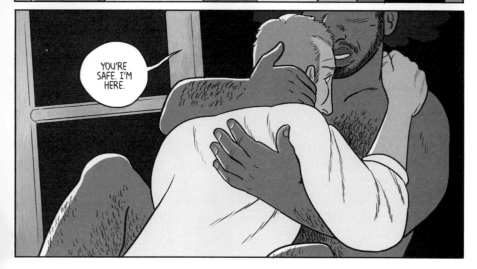

HE'S INSIDE MY HEAD.
HE SEES MY THOUGHTS.
THERE'S NOWHERE I CAN HIDE.
YOU'RE SAFE NOW-
NO.
HE WANTS TO-
HE'S PLAYING WITH MY MIND.
HE CUT ME INTO PIECES.
HE'S SO CRUEL, AND I'M SO SCARED,
AND EVERYBODY ELSE JUST CARRIES ON-
DARLING-
I CAN'T DO THIS, I'M NOT STRONG ENOUGH.
I CAN'T SLEEP, OR EAT, OR CLOSE MY EYES.

ED. YOU DON'T HAVE TO BE STRONG.
THE REST OF THE COURT, EVERYBODY-
EDMUND. NO. NOT AT ALL.
WE ARE ALL SCARED TO DEATH OF HIM.
HE'S A MONSTER.
WE'VE ALL HAD TO LEARN OUR INDIVIDUAL WAYS OF COPING WITH HIM.
DO YOU REMEMBER HOW I CRIED IN THE RITUAL ROOM?

I'M SORRY.
I DIDN'T LET YOU CHOOSE.
I WAS AFRAID-
I'M SORRY.

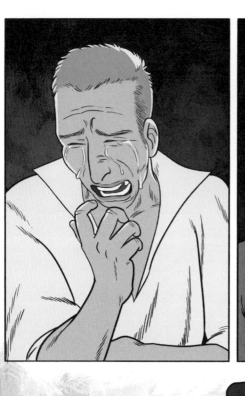

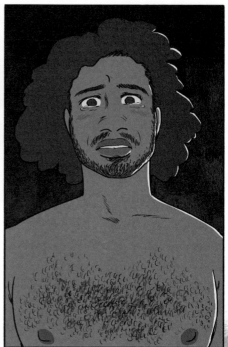

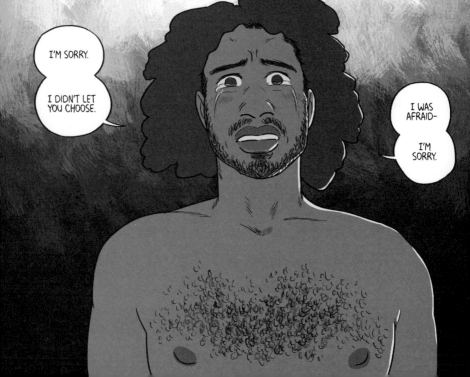

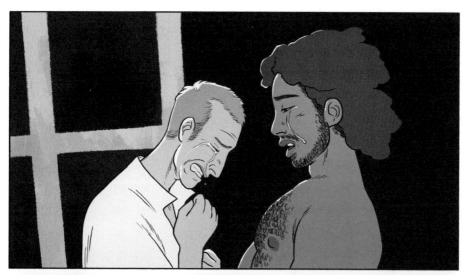

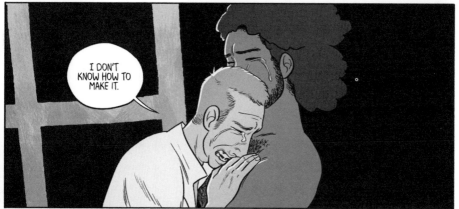

I DON'T KNOW HOW TO MAKE IT.

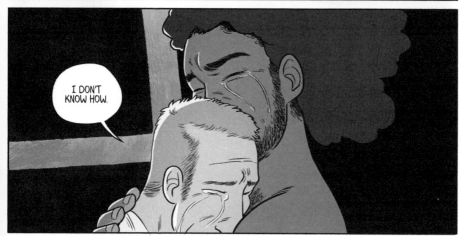

I DON'T KNOW HOW.

131

PLEASE, MY LADIES,
BE CAREFUL IN THE SNOW!

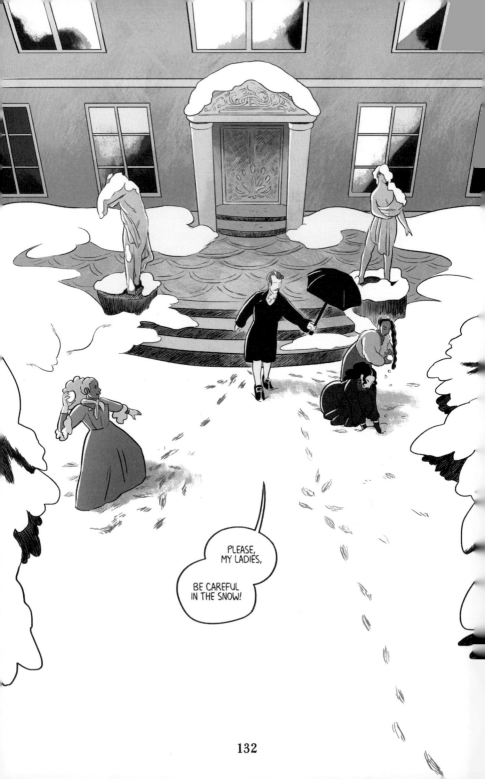

NOW CAN BE
TE AN IRRITANT
ON THE SKIN

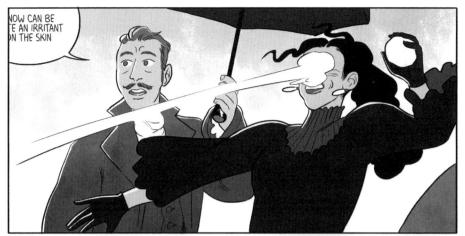

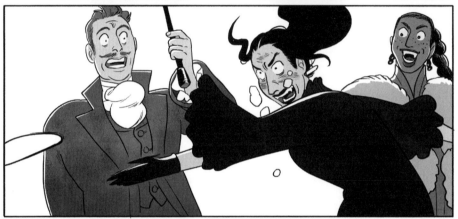

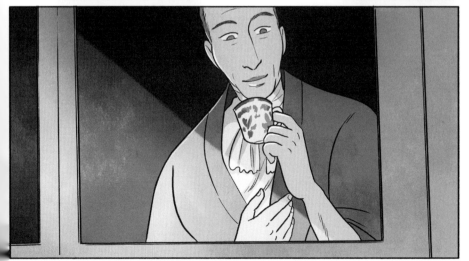

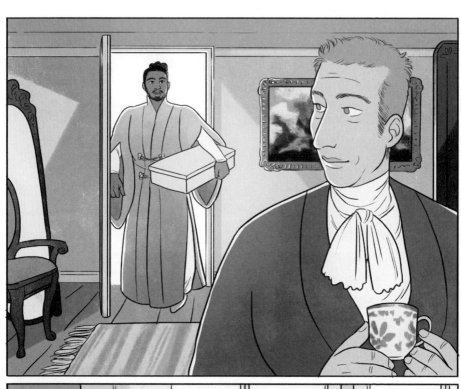

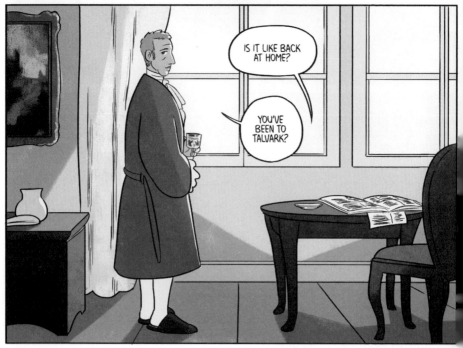

IS IT LIKE BACK AT HOME?

YOU'VE BEEN TO TALVARK?

I HAVEN'T, ACTUALLY.
BUT I KNOW YOU GET SNOW UP THERE.
LESS SO BY THE SEA, OR THE INDUSTRIAL TOWNS.
BUT WHERE I WAS BORN, YES, THERE WAS SNOW EVERY WINTER.

ARE YOU FEELING HOMESICK?
MAYBE.

ONLY A LITTLE, THOUGH.
THERE ISN'T ANYTHING FOR ME TO RETURN TO, IN TALVARK.
WE COULD STILL VISIT SOMETIME, IF YOU WANT.
I'D LIKE TO SEE IT.

YOU CAN DRESS IT UP, OR DOWN...
FOR A MORE CASUAL LOOK.
AM I ALLOWED TO LOOK CASUAL IN THE NIGHT COURT?
HONEY, I'M THE ONE WHO MADE CASUAL FASHIONABLE HERE.

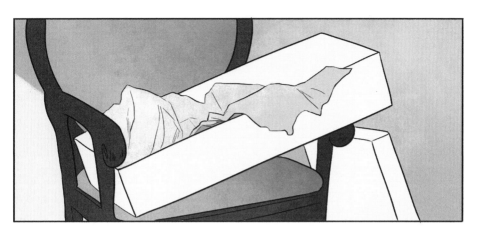

IT'S ABOUT SELF-EXPRESSION.
ONCE YOU PICK UP ALL THE RULES, I ENCOURAGE YOU TO BREAK THEM.

HEY.

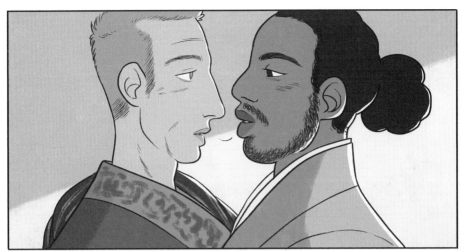

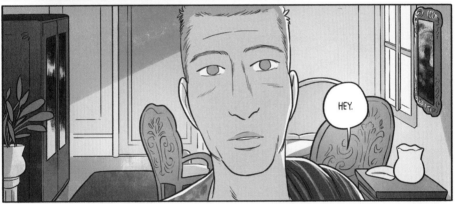

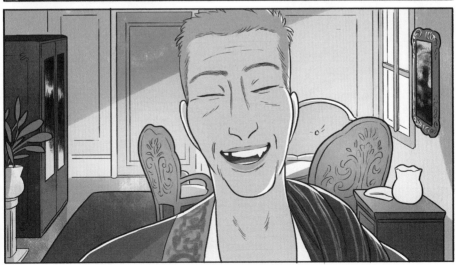

AND THE NATURE IN ITS CRUELTY SAID,
"COME! YOU ARE BORN."
AND WE CRY AS WE ARE BORN,
AS NEITHER A YES OR NO EXISTS TO US.

LIKE DEATH IS VIOLENCE, SO IS LIFE.
FOR A FLEETING MOMENT WE ARE ASKED TO FIND THE BOUNDARY BETWEEN US AND PAIN.

BUT THE SILENT LORD MAY CRADLE US IN HIS ARMS,
AND AS WE HAVE FOUND OUR WORDS, HE MAY ASK:
DO WE NOT DESERVE A PATH BEYOND THE PATH?
AND WE MAY ANSWER:
LET THE NATURE BE UNDONE,
LET THE BOUNDARIES BE UNDONE,
MAY WE BE REBORN FROM HIM.

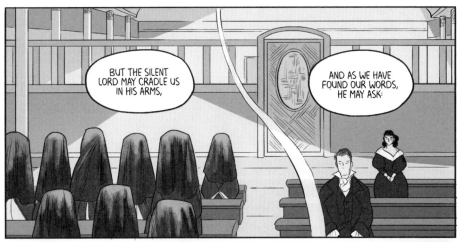

HOW MUCH DO I DRINK?
AS MUCH AS YOU CAN.

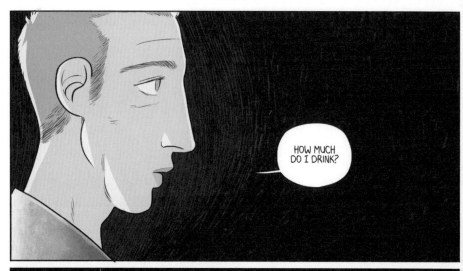

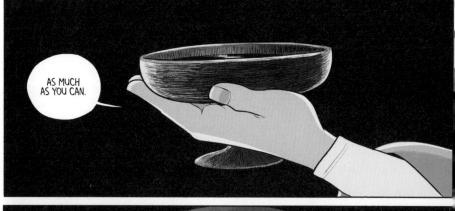

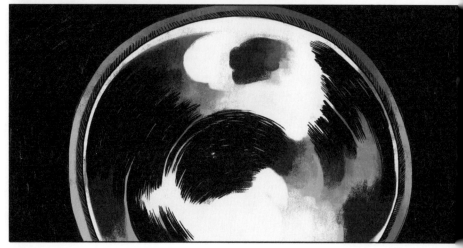

I KEEP THINKING OF WHAT YOU SAID.
HOW DO YOU COPE WITH IT?

WITH HIM?
YES.
AT NIGHT. OR, WHEN YOU'RE ALONE.
OR... WHEN YOU HAVE TO MEET HIM.

I **DON'T**, MOST OF THE TIME.
SEE HIM, OR COPE WITH HIM?
HEH. EITHER.
MOST OF US NEVER TALK TO HIM IF WE CAN HELP IT.
FATHER DOES IT FOR US.
HEAD OF THE FAMILY, AND ALL THAT.
DO YOU THINK...
HE'S HANDLING ALL OF IT WELL?
DEALING WITH THE SILENT LORD ALL BY HIS LONE-SOME, I MEAN.
IBAULD? HE'S THE TOUGHEST PERSON IN THE WORLD.
I KNOW HE LOOKS FRAGILE, BUT THERE'S NOTHING THAT CAN TOPPLE HIM.
HE'LL BE **FINE**.

...
I GUESS YOU KNOW HIM THE BEST.
I LIKE HEARING YOU EXPRESS CONCERN FOR THE OLD MAN, THOUGH.
I SUPPOSE WE'RE TURNING IT AROUND, HIM AND I.

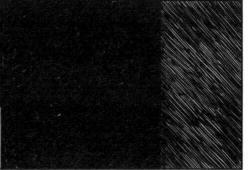

161

RUN AWAY WITH ME.
TONIGHT.
INTO A FOREST NO HUMAN HAS VISITED.
OR TO THE SHADOWS OF A FERTILE FARMLAND, WHERE FOOD NEVER RUNS OUT.

HOW ARE WE TALKING?
WE AREN'T.
WE ARE ONLY SIMPLE BEASTS.
BUT THERE IS ONLY ROOM FOR TRUTH IN OUR HEARTS, NOW.
THE TRUTH OF YOURS AND MINE.

DO YOU
FEEL IT?
OOOOVVVU
UUVVVVVVUUUUUU

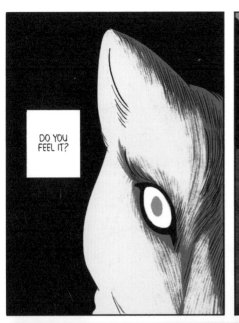

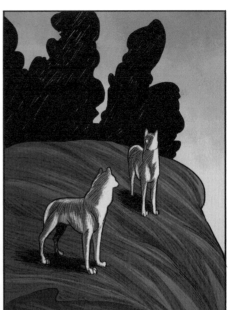

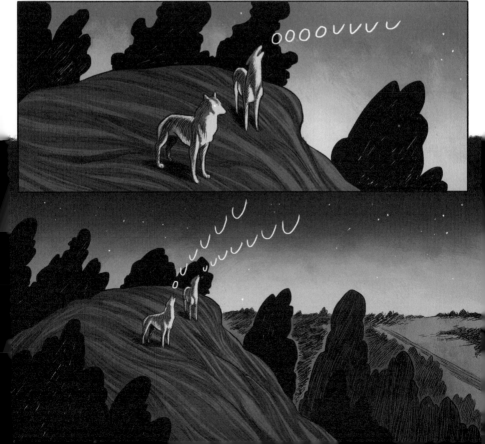

MY MAIDS WOKE ME UP WITH FUNNY GOSSIP THIS MORNING, -
ONE CLAIMS TO HAVE SEEN A PAIR OF WOLVES IN THE GARDENS AT NIGHT.
OH?
YES.
OH.

THAT IS FUNNY GOSSIP.
HOPE-FULLY THE WOLVES WILL TAKE BETTER CAUTION IN THE FUTURE.

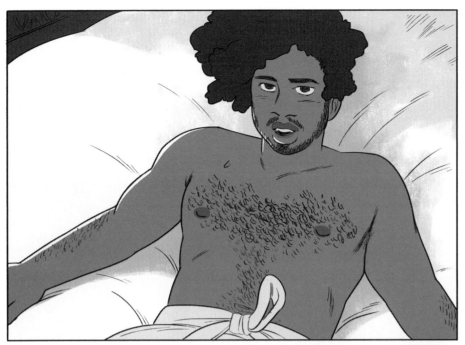

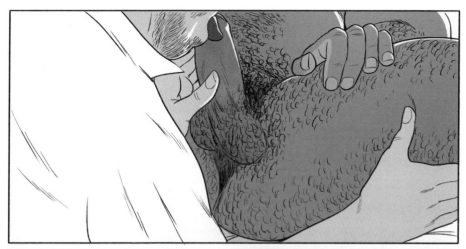

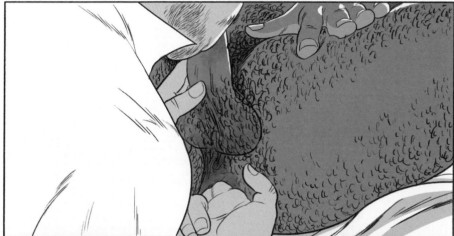

AH
FUCK

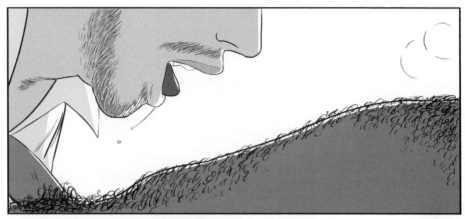

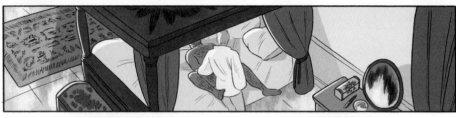

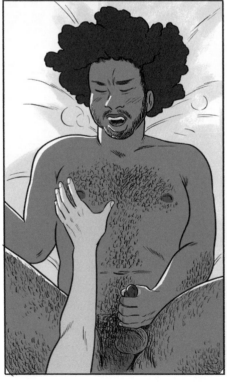

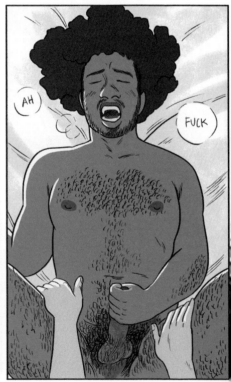

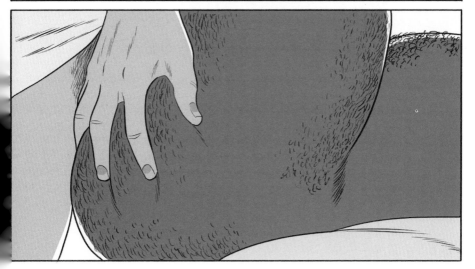

ED
DON'T STOP-
OH
I'M DONE, HONEY.

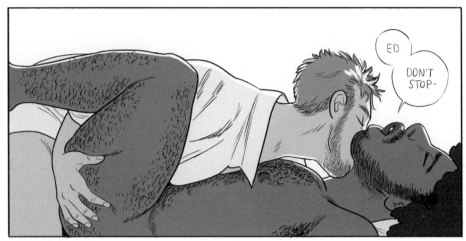

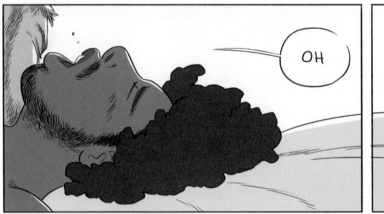

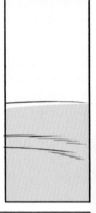

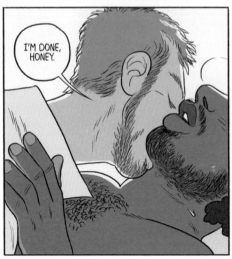

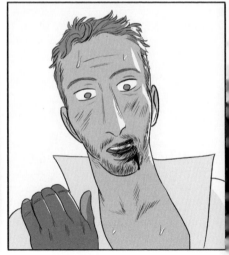

OH, SHIT!
HA HA HA
I DIDN'T MEAN-
WAIT, HONEY-
GET YOUR COCK OUT OF MY ASS AND WE'LL PATCH IT UP.

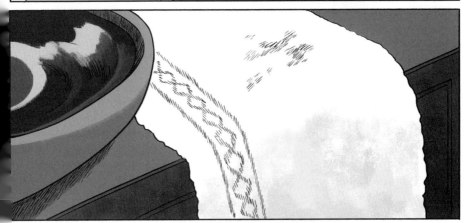

IS IT GOING TO BE OKAY?

OF COURSE IT WILL.
IT'S JUST BLOOD.
IT LOOKED LIKE A LOT.
DON'T WORRY, IF YOU'D NICKED AN ARTERY WE'D **KNOW**.
IT WOULD HAVE BEEN LIKE A PISSING HORSE.

HAHA
RELAX, SWEETIE.
YOU DIDN'T HURT ME.
YOU MADE YOUR MAN COME WITH A LITTLE BLOOD PLAY.
YOU'LL GET OVER IT.
I GUESS IT WAS A LITTLE EXCITING.

DO YOU STILL...
DO I STILL WHAT?
WHAT IS IT?

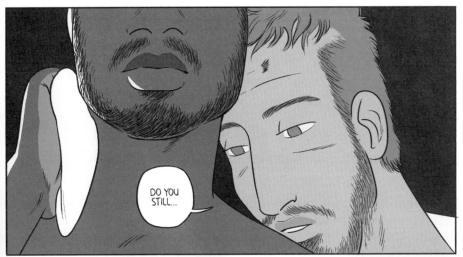

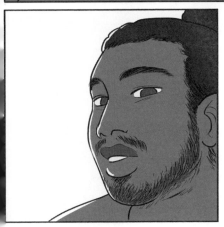

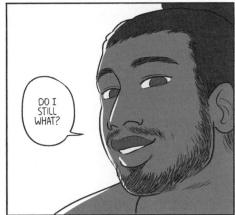

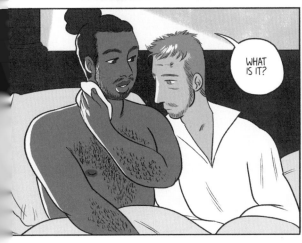

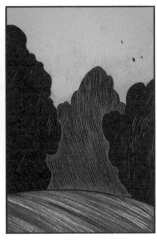

DO YOU STILL WISH TO MARRY ME?

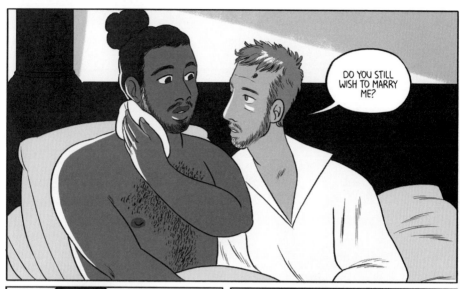

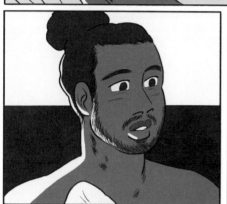

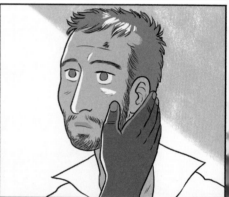

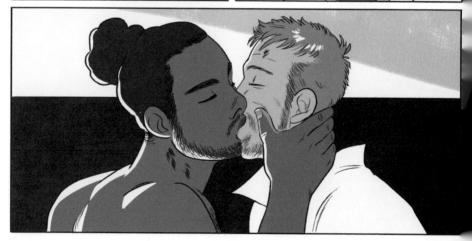

183

185

DO YOU THINK YOU
CAN RUN FROM ME?

IT'S OUR FAVORITE GAME.

YOU RUN, AND RUN, AND RUN.

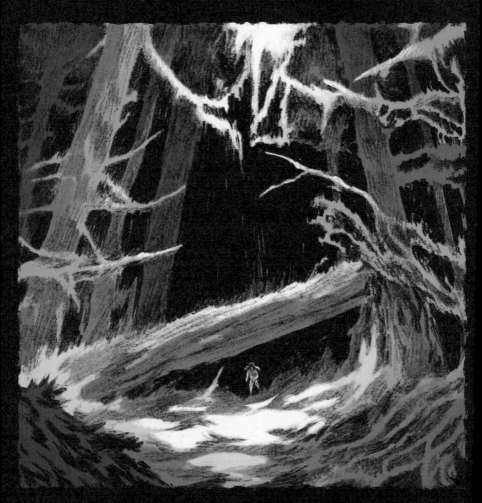

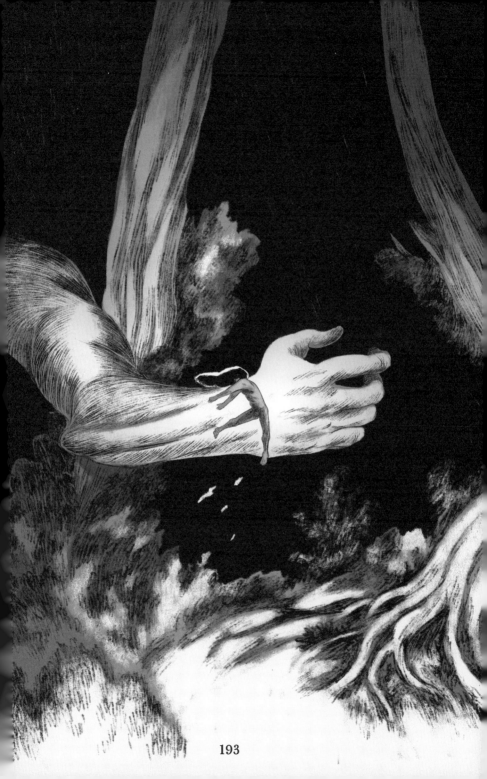

IS THERE SOMEBODY THERE?

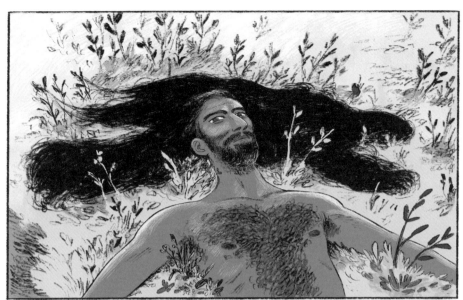

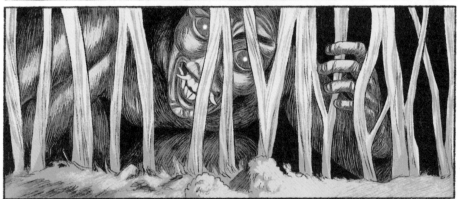

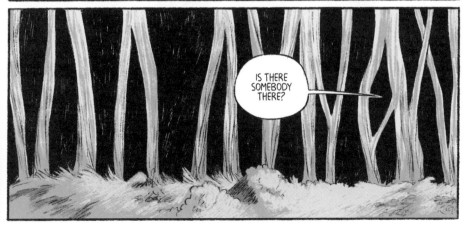

LETTERS FOR LUCARDO
CONCLUDES IN BOOK FOUR

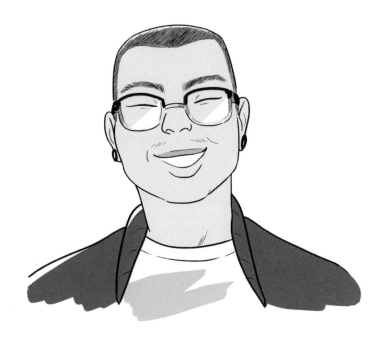

OTAVA HEIKKILÄ (B. 1990) IS A COMIC ARTIST FROM TAMPERE, FINLAND. HIS EARLIER WORKS INCLUDE THE COMICS 'SHATTERED SPEAR', 'SASHA FROM THE GYM', AND SEVERAL SHORT STORIES TO THE ANTHOLOGY SERIES 'SMUT PEDDLER' BY IRON CIRCUS.

OTAVA STARTED WORKING ON THE FOUR-PART COMIC SERIES 'LETTERS FOR LUCARDO' IN 2015, OR APPROXIMATELY A LIFETIME AGO WHEN COUNTED IN WORLD EVENTS. BY THE TIME YOU READ THIS, THE FOURTH AND FINAL BOOK WILL BE UNDER PRODUCTION, - HOPEFULLY THE CONCLUSION WILL BE AS SATISFYING FOR THE READERS AS IT HAS BEEN TO GROW ALONG WITH THIS STORY.